Through the eyes of a trauma child

New And Contemporary Poetry Collection

By
Debra Reay

ISBN:

Dedicated to every single survivor of childhood abuse

To my family

You all give me reasons to keep going and are teaching me every single day what true love means, while you continue to keep me grounded.

To my friends

You never gave up on me, even when I almost gave up on myself. You all believed in me, when I doubted myself.

To my therapist

You held space for me to explore my trauma, with you by my side. You made me realise my worth, have shown care and love and have taught me that I can be my true self. For that, I will be forever grateful to you. Together we created a safe space!

Final word

You have all contributed to this journey, making me the woman I am today.

Each of you will always have a special place in my heart!

So, thank you.

I love you all!

Here, I am sharing a collection of poetry that I have carefully compiled over the course of the last three years.

I am telling my story through a love of words, and I am reaching out, helping other survivors of abuse to believe that they are worthy, too – You are not alone!

You can delve into my world, through my poetry and come through much stronger, knowing that there is hope, there is always hope!

Here you will find some hard stuff but amongst the heart wrenching material, you will find some uplifting, positive and hopeful material.
Here, you will discover hope and strength – from one girl's perspective!

Exploding thunder
Sunshine with downpours of rain
Greeted by rainbows

Acknowledgements

J.D. Greyson - @JDGreysonwrites
Silver - @Silveringrose
Broken Free - @Blackonred
Tres K - @Tysm_poetry
Misplaced comma or Julee Balko when I'm an author -
@Misplacedcomma2
Liz Kyfer - @LizKyfer
Kevin Delaney – Contemporary Poet. Friend -
@junkpoetic
Move Me Poetry - @MoveMePoetry
AnnieB@annieb222
WriteEthan@WriteEthan
JennyStarr@TheJennyStarr
Magnolia@magnolia3169
JameyBoelower@jdog90
ShazGilmore@ShazGilmore
DarrylLovie@DarrylLovie

Christine Garvey – Beta reader and friend, who initially
began this journey alongside me, over 22 years ago as my
midwife!

J.D is the founder of Move Me Poetry and over time her
writing community has grown into an amazing space for all
creators to create! Move Me Poetry has been home to so
many writers worldwide and speaking of my own
experience with Move Me, they have been the stepping
stone of my own success. I joined in 2020 and Jacki took
me under her wing, introducing me to writers and artists,
who welcomed me into their worlds. Not only this but she
has been my biggest cheer leader, loved me and supported
my journey – while being a mother, wife and doing work on
Move Me. She also has a publication on Medium for writers
to publish their work online. Check them out!

A child unloved

From tiny toes to troubled souls
She fought so hard to be heard
Nobody cared for the pain within
A child who was hurt and scarred
Years went by and the pain got bad
A child unloved was a child so sad

She pulled away from what she knew
But they pulled her in some more
The more she fought, the worse it got
The adults she knew didn't stop
Her body scarred was no longer hers
A child unloved was a child no more

What they did was too bad to tell
Besides, who would believe this girl
More years went by for this poor girl
More damage and pain endured
When will it end so she can live
A child unloved was a child so hurt

The child grew up and got away
The torture left behind
But she struggled with life
And her place in the world
Her story didn't end there
A child unloved was a child so dear

Her next big struggle was a bottle of wine
And pills to dull the pain
She carried on, no care in the world
Self-destruction was her middle name
Depressed and alone was this lost soul
A child unloved was a child unknown

Her family gone, no fault of her own
Her life in bits but she's to carry on
She built her life, little by little
A smile can be seen on her pale face
And a little sadness behind her green eyes
A child unloved was unloved no more

To thrive alone

Standing alone
And growing
In keeping your soul as busy
And the memories at arm's length
To grow
In beauty
You thrive

In a tempest of beaten storms

In a tempest of
Beaten storms
Her trauma
To break her down
Yet build her up
Voiceless
She utters
Wisdom
And to falter
Is to have
No option
To survive
Yet, the tempest
Beaten with
The last word
I'm not the trauma you
Created, but the warrior I
Grew and fought to become

Displaced love

An abundance of
A displaced love
With no openings
Of arms to hold her
While her beating heart
Is in distress
And a voyage of pain
Inflicted upon
Her inner cries
Yet, transparent tears
She sits sullenly
Weeping as she waits
For her next wave of euphoria

Unkept promises

You beat her fragile soul
Yet you told her no more
You acted like nothing was wrong
As she cowered on the floor
A promise meant nothing
A field of beauty
Of wildflowers and dreams
Her dreams shattered
By your words of
Unkept promises
A thousand times embedded
Within her brain
She hears those words
Of a thousand
Unkept promises

Returning her to Sixteen

Meeting of eyes
Interlocking his
Power to her fear
Returning her to Sixteen
Her heart fades
She sees through her own flaws
Blaming herself
But what why?
Returning her to Sixteen
Dreaming of an end
Yet, not even close
Rocking in corners
She sighs…
It's over
Nearly of an age
Of knowing her own mind
Yet, overloaded with fear
On her own
Lost and invisible
Returning her to Sixteen

Peace

Distant fog
Peaceful wonder
As the sunsets on mountain tops
Therapeutically woven, Sunday walks in June
To love
Fresh air
And breath

Somewhere in-between

Between hope and fear
Crossing portal to portal
Stands a figure of stillness
Of broken spirits – unfixable
While a dare to dream
In wavering eternities
Pulling in the direction of
Somewhere in-between
A road untaken
And a path afraid to cross
An existence, a life
A choice for better
For more than survival
From somewhere in-between

Never leave her to dwell

Never leave her to dwell
But leave her for only a while
Let her gather her thoughts
And let her know you are there
Do not promise her the world
Then decide to walk away
She will hold onto your every word
Just, never leave her to dwell
But leave her for only a while

Letting go

In sorrow, surrendering
A lost love, in lightness
Desiring and desperate
To let go of what has gone
But how?
Clambering, calmly to her feet
She bows, begging for forgiveness
Owning her part, her offering
To a sense of blame and betrayal
But why?
A sense of self worthlessness
Letting go of lost love
A challenge, a call to her inner self
Permission to pour these words
It's time to let go

Do not come for me

Do not come for me
From a space over yonder
As I set sail
My thoughts
And lose the rumblings
Of my word spewn mind
Do not come for me
Destroying all that I built
A fort of a sanctuary
With walls as big
As the memories inside
Just do not come for me
Leave me within these walls

You took from me

You took from me
A mother – a love
A child's dream
Safety
Security
You told me why
Yet – did you lie
You told me too little
Reasons hard to see
Hard to believe
A struggle etched in me
How can I grieve
For someone I didn't have
A mother who is living

Without a trace

You absconded
Leaving not a trace
Thrown from the frying pan
And into the fire
Yet you didn't know
Maybe you didn't care
A big hole left, unfilled
And untouched
Lasting damage
Like a trainwreck, which
Can slowly rebuild
Yet different
Craving a mother's love
Memories unseen
And left invisible

Broken spirit

All the beatings, her
Trials and tribulations
Spirits scorned – broken
By the wronguns
Defying all odds
She survived, yet
Not from beatings
But of a desire
To live
And to be alive
Re-building what
You sabotaged
Fixing her broken spirit

Words

Words fuelled by anger
She searches for a way out
There's always a way

Unfelt cracks

Cracks lost in mildew
Broken pieces of me
Stilled and untouched
Poisoned by something
Or nothing – yet tainted
Rocking in the stillness
Of shadows behind the
Unfelt cracks of my soul
Waiting in solitude
Fragments of my soul
Missing or misplaced
Lost beneath the layers
Of each crack – greeted
By tiny threads of my
Imagination, no less
A dream, a reality
Memory or just hope
A hope for better
As cracks slowly repair
Paving the way for more…hope

Spirits and Moonlights

Moonlights
Intertwining
Stars shining
Letting go of
What's gone
Before us
Echoed in silence
To bode well
When the heart swells
Yet broken
Are the spirits of moonlights
On dark nights
As the stars guide us
Into an intertwining of
Lights and moonlights

Re(tired)

Re(tired)
Is not old nor useless
But scarred and free
A burial of pain
Inflicted within
The deepest
Part of her being
Her mind spews
Volcanic acid – like
Her thoughts too painful
They erupt until nothing left
Re(tired)
Is not old nor useless
Abused and stomped on
Flesh peeled back
Scarred, yet alive
Mind erupting
With words spewing
Like volcanic acid
Stepping back
Into her own realities
She is not old nor useless – but
Re(tired)

Memories

Fluorescent unearthed
Memories unravelling
Like pandora's box

As beautiful as acapella

Take me to a place
That I dream of
Where beauty is
Around every corner
And hatred is non-existent
Where children play and sing
As beautiful as acapella
Take me to a place
To call my own
Where the sea breeze
Sweeps away our troubles
And life is perfect
Where music plays
As beautiful as acapella

Uncried tears

Uncried are the tears
Buried are the emotions
Afraid to speak up or tell
Of her feelings no longer silent
Time is hers, to start living
Gone are the days of fear
Uncried are the tears
As the world learns
Of her truths
To face her fears
And unhide her emotions
As she tells her story
Through uncried tears

Just a girl

I am that girl
Abandoned
Rejected and
Disowned
Born into chaos
A seeker
An all-in kind of girl
You see – I love
Given the chance
Though, you leave
You all left
I am that girl
Searching
Learning
And longing
Surviving you
A seeker
Of acceptance
A wisher
Of a place to belong
I am that girl

I ask, not for truth

I ask, not for truth
But a freedom to tell
In a hidden valley of tears
Falling in open fields
Of wildflowers
A place where things
Stay hidden amongst
Furled petals of velvet
And the remains of
Secrets buried and untouched
I ask, not for truth
But a strength to tell my story
In this valley of tears
Which fall in open fields
Of wildflowers

If I had my time again

If I had my time again
I'd tell you no
A million knots louder
I would fight back
While my words would matter
You would be stunned
If I had my time again
I'd tell all and sundry
To make people listen
To my words unspoken, I'd tell
My body language
Would speak
Along with my voiceless whispers
If I had my time again
I would stop you all
Yet, no bruising present
Though, you'd be held accountable
Justice would come knocking
And I'd have had a life
If I had my time again
I would live in peace
As a child, I'd play
Learn and grow
I would live without shame
Be fearless of the world
If I had my time again

The unspoken word

She sits with sadness behind her smile
On a pedestal
Like in a fashion show
With only you as her audience
Unable to cry
Or shed a single tear
Stripped of her innocence
With a powerful word
Shared with only she
Her life nothing
Worthless, she feels
Words and threats
Ringing through her ears
With nobody to save her
Not a single person to care
Her life hopeless
Yet through sheer desperation
She finds courage to stand up
And finally say
Enough

The bearer of my soul

I watched from within my walls
Where fear is the bearer of my soul
A badness forms what might be seen
Yet more hatred becomes the norm
I watched from my tear-filled eyes
As torture was all I knew
Hiding once more behind my mask
I stand tall, yet in disguise and ready
To allow my strength
And beat down the walls of my fear

Like a phoenix

Like a phoenix
She rises taller
And stronger
Than all those
Who wronged her
Her soul killed
And destroyed
Yet each time reborn
Each time stronger
Like a phoenix
She rises
Never beaten down
A war she never lost
The battle to survive
Like a phoenix, she lives

Winsome smiles

Wear winsome smiles
Shine shimmering and sweetly
Stand strong with sparkle

You see me

You see me
Through powerful eyes
Through my weakness
You see me
Look at me fly
Through a strength
You never thought I had
Rolling with the punches
Your punches and brutal truths
Sorrow built
As the walls rise
Can you see me
A woman who climbs mountains
Who escaped you
Look at me now
As I change my world
My Independence Day came
When you failed to see me
I ran as I learned to live
Where I transformed

Hold her in the light

When she let you in
She let you close
Just to get her fingers burnt
You lied and held her in silence
Afraid to speak truth
As she battled with demons
Berated by you – beaten down
Words of simple hate
A trusting heart as hers
Beating rhythmless
Naming you all
A task too much to fulfil
And a pain too deep
Don't make her let you in
Just to get her fingers burnt
Give her a trust
And hold her in the light

Her reflection

Mirrored reflections
Standing in admiration
Just look at her now

Who will read my eulogy

Who will read my eulogy when I die
Says the mind of a child
Thrown away like garbage
Who will be at my wake
Or weep at my graveside
Who will miss me when I'm gone
Say the words of nobody
A promise to myself when I died
Words written on scraps of paper
And left by my coffin for the crows to hide

Who will read my eulogy when I die
A stranger who only knows my name
Who may only see my empty shell
A stranger who shares my name
Inscribed upon a memory shared
Don't come and weep fake tears
Only speak my name with fondness
An empty church with empty pews
Who will read my eulogy in an empty room
I am the ghost of she –
Who wrote her own eulogy

Pick me from the ashes

In the morning hush
As temptations turn
To desperation
My mind throbbing
With painful nurturing
Of words spoken
Yet unheard
In the silenced minds
Closed eyes
Dreaming of moments
A trigger is pulled
Pain less, not painless
Pick me from the ashes
Of a smoke-filled flash
Though…
My time here
Just beginning
Dreams fulfilling
In the morning hush
I sit at peace
With moments
Passing by
In a wilderness
Of painless thoughts
When my times comes
Pick me from the ashes

Today's sometimes

There are those times
The sun rises and sets
Over misty meadows of somewhere
And the shimmering of waters calm
Sometimes the heart will dance
To happy tunes or cry in sorrow
When we cannot look beyond our flaws
Today's sometimes the heart tries
Protesting it's love to all who give
All my sometimes
I try, my heart will give
To all who needs it
Today's sometimes my heart receives
Not pain but a love to be treasured
Today's sometimes the heart, my heart
Will keep beating the beat
Of precious life and beauty

I did not shrivel, I did not die

You thought you could destroy me
That my beauty would shrivel and die
You told the world I failed to really see

The world as cruel as you made it
After each touch upon my being
Sour words that left your lips
My life, you said had no meaning

I did not really shrivel or die
I went away to gain my strength
To out your every lie
Yes, I went to every length

Like a flower, I blossom
I lay myself out in full glory
A flower that cannot be forgotten
While I'm here to tell my story

I did not shrivel
I did not die

Mum

Goodbye
To the woman
Who birthed me
Yet didn't want me
I cried for you
In my lowest moments
I needed you
Though, you did not come
Today is goodbye
Tomorrow in silence
I grieve for the mother
I wished you had become
Wishing day through night
For a chance to be yours
To feel safe in your grip
But in life
Your heart is closed
A dream is to hope
A hope is to wish
But my wish didn't come true
Did you nurture the baby I was?
Wiping away my tears
Or singing me lullabies?
I have questions
Owing to you
To the woman
Who birthed me
Now, my time has come
To say goodbye

A world in cupped hands

I want to
Hold a world
In cupped hands
Out of harm's way
To save a world
Taking chances
Shelter a universe
Taking away a pain
Deeply embedded
Within souls
Destroying each
Fibre of a being
I want to
Keep safely
Your safety
Picking up
The remnants
Of a shattered soul
Seeing clearly
It takes more
Than one to
Hold a world
In cupped hands
To bless and be blessed
And to save just one
I want to…

A taste of purity

Tears flow
Shiny glow
As they roll down her cheeks
Heart palpitations, as she sighs silently
Sweet whisperings
Somebody's listening
At last

Everyday I'm searching…

I want to see my worth
And to feel that I'm worthy
Go beyond a wildest dream
That I'm deserving of more
I listen with a broken heart
Seeing through a blinded lens
Everyday I'm searching…

Lies that you made me believe
Truths you dismissed
Nobody would ever care
Your words in my ear
Everyday I'm searching…

As you whispered hatred
Telling would render you a liar
The fear driven from your voice
Had me searching deep inside my soul
Everyday I'm searching…

Am I worth it
Will I feel worthy
Beyond my wildest dreams
Am I deserving of more because
Everyday I'm searching...

Catch me

Teach me
Show me
How to heal from this stuff
Please catch me before I fall
Help me
To survive
This life

Stay

You heard
My cries
But chose to ignore my pain
Deep cuts to my precious soul
Don't run
Away again
Just stay

Not my superpower

Amongst brain matter
As oxygen and blood flow
Haplessly divine
Fighting the voices
Existing only in one's mind
Each fibre – push and pull, pressure
Echoing reaching comfort
Non existing – treasure
You are not my superpower
A mind as ruined as hers
As words spew into confusion
Amongst brain matter
Lay dormant
Peace and tranquillity
Interrupted by chaos
Colours twisting
Running, Red – Blue
The way she is feeling
You are not my superpower
As she disappears inwards – replaying
You are not my superpower

The ruler in her

The ruler of her history
As a healer of time
She fought battles
Made up in your mind

Though real to her
A bravery unseen
In shadows dark
Hiding her beauty

One thing you should know
The time and the place
Is the where's and the why's
Then to picture his face

Forget all the fears
All the negative traits
He damaged you for years
Don't let the bastards berate – YOU!

Free

It's Baltic in here
Blooming blossoms born
Into winters freeze
While chaotic minds run wild
Amidst oceans rumblings
Drowning in tears
She frees the mind
Setting sail the chaos
While looking death
Square in the face

A pledge

Look inside of you
Search for the love
You store for rainy days
Your safe as houses
Forty-nine years stolen
A childhood gone
Her sweet innocence
Eaten up and spat out
Today, she takes a leap of faith
A deep breath, a sigh of relief
As she reaches for the stars
Dreaming big
Bigger than those who wronged her
Look inside of you
Little by little
Take down that wall
Holding you back
Make a pledge
Only you will understand
Inside of you
Lies authenticity
A true warrior woman
Ready to take a world by storm

Tis the night

Tis the night before Christmas
The world slows to a halt
Sounds disappear
And the striking of midnight ceases
Children sleeping by eight
Not but one
A child's cry
In distant skies
Tears fall upon
Ice-bitten ground
As she wanders
She waits
Stumbling upon
Words and stutters and fear
Raising of fists
Or slaps across the face
Forced into darkness
Tis the night before Christmas
A time for rejoicing
I look deeply into
The eyes of a child
Who does not smile
Why does she not smile?
This is a child lost
Lost in a cycle of terror
Striving to find her place
Spending a lifetime fighting
Before her life ends…She fights

Beginnings

An intertwining
Of our soulful beginnings
This is what matters

Darling

Whispers weaving wholesomely
Through a transparency of trees
Secrets silenced by changing seasons
Her aching hearts hopeless
Yet –
Dreaming, darling of happier times
She stands in a picturesque of beauty
As she keeps moving forward
In moments
Of time stood still

A dare to dream

In
Oceans
Calm ripples
Thoughts separate
Floating to and fro
As waves crash fearlessly
Her thinking's unorganised
As she grabs with both hands, to life
Drowning in panic-stricken waters
Eye sealed closed as her body floats solo
Silver linings appearing untouched
A dare to dream of letters sent
With words, notes, and emotions
Setting sail a thousand
Whispers and tears cried
Today's sunrise
Positive
Words set
Sail

Crossing rainbows

A rainbow once spoke to me
Inviting me to cross
It echoed in subtle whispers
Come dear, I see that you are lost
I imagined it as calm
As beautiful as it was
I couldn't bring myself to cross
I don't think I was ready
I still had a lot of work to do
A rainbow who knew my fears
Who said, I would never judge you
I admit that I was lost
The fear instilled within me
That I almost forgot
My place in the world
Since the rainbow spoke my name
I haven't heard that subtle whisper
I found my place and my head is in the game

From the cracks, I fall

Falling between the cracks
Of a broken lens
Failed reflections
Familiar selections
Of a lost love
Resting in heaven above
On clouds where angels rest
And birds build their nests
Falling once more
Through the crack
Of an open door
One more day, I say
Death is the only way

Times of brokenness

During times
Of brokenness
Spurs on a rollercoaster of emotions
Provoking thoughts and feelings that collide
You fought
For life
And won

Answers

Her mind collides
With tidal waves
Beating against her
For answers
Like thunder beating
Against the clouds
And fire beating
Against life
What answers?
Where does she seek
To know where to look
Beneath her fear
As deep as her soul allows
Lay untouched – sacred
Answers buried

Picking up the pieces

Picking up the pieces
Of shattered
Souls scattered
Across frost bitten soil
Crunches underfoot
Freshly settled
Like a wish to become so
But no…
She is shattered
Into a million pieces
Her body present
With her soul hesitant
Of trying, crying
A piece of her forgotten
Seen but cannot unsee
What stands before her
Demons overriding minds
Capturing and unearthing
A mourning shell of herself
While picking up
A million pieces of her soul

The ole shack

Abandoned piles of wood
Thrown together
As an ole shack
Disguised and derelict
Yet secrets held
Within these walls
Her silent cries
Muffled by her fists
Left alone for hours
In the company
Of her thoughts
And the darkness
Of her mind
Sanity relinquished
She rendered her
Strength and courage
Found in the essence
Of her survival in
The ole shack

Season's dread

As winter is nearing
As winter's dread
Where families gather
As they rejoice as one
Then there is me
Frightened and alone
Though, not quite alone
Stuck in a time of
Desperation
A date and time
A year tattooed on my soul
An anniversary
Best forgotten
But how?
I almost died that day
Yet you didn't stop
Allowing for your audience to watch
Here, my season's dread lives

Look for the light

In times of restrained
Where uncertainty is fear
Now look for the light

Wildflower

I yet but wander
Through the fields
Of sweet-smelling wildflower
Anchoring by thoughts
Of beauty and elegance
Each stem rests tall
As the sun beams down
Upon each flower
Leaving not a single
Soul behind

I am not a woman scorned

Exposed to a world
Of inhumanity and torture
You scorned me – yet
I am not a woman scorned
My mind turned frail
Like wilted flowers
Trodden on and berated
Dark souls you created
Damning you made me
An object of your own desires
You scorned a child, come woman
Who grew to realise
How immortal you deemed to be
Yet you became unstuck
In your ventures to destroy
Your own offspring
Your child – yet
I had the last laugh
I gained solidarity
Courage to carry on
And a legacy to all survivors

Honour the love

Love thyself
The now's
The past
And the future
Honour the love
You couldn't hold
What is love?
How do we learn?
And from whom?
Unanswered
Unborn knowledge
All that is known
We are all worthy
Of a love
And forgiving hearts
Unfavoured
And an
Unswayed love
In fields filled with daisies
A beauty only you can see
Yet a love we can all feel

There are no winners

I could not win the race
Of times stopped
In winter's flavours
Violins pause strumming
Down to the core
My body frozen
Through fear – yet
My soul is sacrificing
During a symphony
Of unheard sounds
A race through
Cascading rituals
Graves digging as
Bells ring aloud
My heart slowly
Withdraws from life
As colour begins to drain
And, life no longer present, as
There are no winners

Climbing mountains

In a fearful world
She climbs mountains with courage
Fearlessly she flies

The lass from the North

Flying solo
Hearts happy dance
Seasons of foreverness
You created a weakless
Lass from the North
Someone who lives
In nobody's shadow
Despite your best efforts
To weaken her soul
The lass from the North
Fly's solo
With reasons to carry on

Revenant

Digging deep into
The soul of a woman
Tortured – yet
Unafraid by what she sees
Her mind splattered
By the harshness of betrayal
As he toyed with a memory
From beneath his grave
A revenant of her past
Of his villainous ways
That should be stamped out
Fought against and destroyed
Digging deep
Into the heart of a woman
Who almost died
Yet who survived
The torture bestowed upon her
By you – The revenant of her past

Her Christmas wish

Fire
Burning
Flames flicker
Laughter and jokes
Can be heard next door
As she sits silently
A daydream of family
Her wish to be loved
A dream means she'd be better off dead
She did not give them the satisfaction

Our embodiment

You
Capture
The spirit
Of fulfilment
Embodied in us
Determination as
Undestroyed profiting lapse
Setting our beauty aside
We fought back and gave in to nothing
We are gifted with our own embodiments

December's wish

December snow falls
Ice crunch trodden
Beneath her feet
Snow angels by children
Perfection through
The freshness of snow
December icicles
Form perfect shapes
Hanging from
Rooftops and trees
Raindrops made icicles
Snowball fights
And hot chocolate
This is a child's life
Through the years
Not mine

I am warrior

Walking through worlds
Shards of unearthed debris
Underfoot, yet carry on
Stronger, broken –
I am warrior
Breaking each layer
Of fragile skin
Like old tatty leather
Torn and scratched –
I am warrior
Daylight falls
Streetlights light up
Like a halo around my head
I stand tall in pretence –
I am warrior
A never-ending journey
Walking through worlds
Stronger, broken but –
I am strength
I am courage
I am hope
I am warrior

Sacred hearts

Offering oneself on
A whim of desperation
To free herself from
A bribe and separation
Expecting the unexpected
She lays sacred
Her heart, body, and soul
Waiting, she waits
Pausing as to hope
Of endings to things
That alter her mind
She survives, yet
Unexpectedly

To the man

To the man who
Ripped out my heart
Who took my soul
To the woman who
Yelled and cursed
Who beat me black and blue
The moon listened
To my whispering cries
At night as darkness fell
Streetlights flicker – a sign?
As though to protect
Keeping those lights on
Awakening my soul
A fight between light and dark
To save me or kill me
I changed that night
I changed the night
The moon listened
I asked to be taken
From the dangers in here
And here I am
No longer dying
Yet here I stand
The night I changed

Freedom

A need for freedom
Let her be free of your grip
Her fear is real

Running free

Like a whistling in the wind
Her voice begins to break
Her fighting spirit visible
Others see her as weak
Though this is not her
She is feisty
Like a lioness
Eyes like daggers
In turn, she will fight
She will win against those
Who did her wrong
She can run free
Without limitations

A wynorrific paradise

Rainforests come alive
Seeing rainbows
Glow within
The fragility of her soul
Seeking peace and tranquillity
A place of solace
Yet her pain and fear too strong
To bare her fallen tears
Cuts to her hands
And feet raw
Like a knife edge
Of her shattered life

An unwritten letter

She ponders cautiously
Thinking in timeless motions
Of her creative streak
Of her next move
From this moment
To the next phase
Ridding of a sin
Beholding her
An evil act against her
Previously be filled with hope
Her desire to leave – yet
Not before having her last say
It goes like this…

"You did your best
To destroy my world
You took me, shred by shred
Peeling back my soul
A layer at a time
Until there was nothing left
You thought you had won
That I would die inside
You were wrong
I'm here alive and surviving"

Those were her last words
Written with your blood
As she makes her next move

Sometimes

Sometimes life
Throws us in directions
We are not ready for
Our lives nurture
In ways we can't understand
Sometimes life is perfect
While others, chaotic
The wind blows while the sun shines
Lightning strikes and bolts of thunder hit
Sometimes our light goes out
And re-ignite within our hearts
Curiously broken
Souls left in pieces
Like ashes afloat
Sometimes life is too hard
Death seems easy
A way to escape
Day becomes night
A week, a month, and a year
Times lost in conflict
Decades pass us by
While memories fade in time
Yet – Sometimes life must be fulfilled
Just, sometimes

Visions

Only through cracked lens
Silhouettes form
Intangible images
Groundless
Familiar stances
A vision seen
Only in her dreams

I look back

I look back
For a moment
To remember
A fear you embedded
So deeply inside of me
I'd need a chisel
To chip away
To free the soul
You took from me
Moments lost
Each beating
Every time
You forced yourself
Upon me
Lost in time
And innocence
The scars on my soul
Unhealed
Your words of vileness
Like a knife
A cut through
Each layer of my being
I look back
For a moment
To try and forget
How each of you made me feel
In all those moments
I look back one more time

Did it really matter?

What's the matter?
The scars upon my soul
The way you made me feel
Too much skin on show

What's the matter?
The way I cowered in a corner
As I waited for the next punch
The tears I cried as day turns to night

What's the matter?
As I begin to fade
And my heart begins to stop
Then people cried as they said goodbye

What's the matter with who I was?
You didn't really cry for the one you killed

Becoming free

Million whispers
Disappearing footsteps
Her pleas fall on deaf ears
As tears roll down her face
Desperate attempts
To run
Becoming free

Am I enough

Am I enough –
A cry for truth
Or dare to feel whole
Am I enough –
A smile in hopes
Miracles here and there
Am I enough
A chancer
Dreamer of dreams
Yet –
I'm not enough
You said
I should die
You wished me dead
I'm not enough
I cry for wholeness
No place to capture
No memories
No return
Yet –
I am enough

Unconquerable

Does it make you hard
Unconquerable
To ridicule a child
To beat her
Leaving her bruised
Yet, you rejoiced
Did she?
She was not weak
Yet but just a child
Nor was she a punching bag
But you made her into one
You say, they made you do it
They did but you could have stopped it
The thrill in your hands
Of whom you almost killed
You think it made you hard
Unconquerable

Hard truths

It's a hard sell
Telling a truth
So deeply buried
Like opening a can of worms
Or pandora's box
With hidden secrets
A potential to destroy them
But didn't
An arrest without a charge
But I am safe
I left before
I told the truth
They say I lied
That I made it up
It's a hard sell, telling the truth
Yet, a truth had to be told
My world destroyed
But I had to tell the hard truth
Then move away
To repair my scars
While placing the lid back
Onto pandora's box

Scolded

You left me scolded
By the words
You let seep from your lips
You inflicted pain
And suffering
Hardships and misery
With each breath you took
You couldn't care less
Of the damage you caused
It gave you power
While you took mine
Pleading for help
As I begged you to stop
Fell upon deaf ears
You left me scolded
Until I could barely breathe
Yet, I'm still here
Unbeaten and alive
You tried and failed
No longer scolded
By the words
You let seep from your lips

Kaleidoscope

Looking through the kaleidoscope
Of hope
She warms to the beauty
Surrounding her
The colour of her soul
Yet, her belief fades
Disbelief that she can breathe
A breath of fresh air
Entering her lungs
She has the last laugh
Whilst others sit on their lies
Her ultimate battle
To be honoured with
A warriorship

In her salvation

In darkness
She weeps
Stars glowing
Her life ruined – yet
In her salvation
She is left wondering
What stands before her
Whilst evil stands between her
And the voices in her head
She craves humanity
To allow her life
To be filled with peace
She fights with all her might
For the life she deserves

Raindrops

To fall from open skies
Or tears that have been cried
Raindrops fall like silent screams
The screams of my inner child
Stop the raindrops falling
The pain I'm enduring
But one thing is for sure
The raindrops will keep falling

The soul of a child

In turbulence
Sweeping
Windy minds blowing
As thundering
Drums pounding
Hard against
The soul of a child
Lightning strikes
Guiding the way
In the direction
Of turbulent winds
A light must shine brightly
As we begin
To change the world
Little by little

The haunting

Her memories
Once failed her
Until one day
A tune, a smell
Where nightmares
Are something else
No longer a blur
While her body stunned
Stuck in a trance
In times stood still
Through her eyes
Where only
Haunted memories reside
Right now
These memories
Are of her soul

Empty chairs

Empty chairs
In subtle airs
Her soul
Overlooking
Murky waters
Where bricks and mortar
Once stood
A shell of emptiness
Of nothingness
As she once sat in peace
Yet – Now she lay
In sweet paradise
Pain-free
Full of life, in her death

There was a place

There was a place
Not so far from my mind
Of lucid calm tones
Whistling of winds blowing
And the falling of leaves
On hardened ground
Underfoot
Rivers and streams
Waterfalls and springs
Of beauty
There was a place
Like the ones I dream of
Where terror did not exist
In this crazy world
No lies nor secrets held
In the quietness of my mind
Inhaling the beauty and
Exhaling in peacefulness
Listening to nature –
There was a place – right here

Two sides

In the face of adversity
Speaking in a tone
Of her wisdom
She seeks solace
Speaking of promise
And faces not but alone
Her attitudes
Of in-between
Two sides
Of living and dying
Alive or not
To survive
Or waiver her right
To life, barely begun
There are always
Two sides of everything

The unwrapping

The unwrapping
Trauma – bitten
Broken hearts equating to damaged souls
As she bleeds ink to paper
Silently sitting
As the
Ink runs

The little girl in yellow bows

I'm sorry I wasn't good enough
To be your perfect little girl
You told me every single day
That I was not fit to be on earth

I have the scars to tell my tail
Of all that you did to me
I grew in fear of who you were
You were killing me, you see

I often sit in aimless wonder
Of why you hated me so
I was just a little girl
With her hair in yellow bows

A memory came flooding in
Of a beating you made me take
You must have really hated me
As you wished me dead, for goodness' sake

You never told me sorry
As you were not good enough
I needed to feel wanted
Yet you couldn't even love

Beauty

There is beauty
To be seen in everything
We just have to look

Undamaged

A once damaged soul
Spending a lifetime searching
Today she finds peace

Secrets of the dark

Living in the shadows
Of shattered silence
Harbouring secrets of the dark
Rattled voices – a struggle
Escalating into hushed lips
Living in the shadows
Of painful memories
Of her past – her fear
In moments of disrepair
And beating hearts collide
She struggles to fight for survival
In life or death, she poises
Fighting each punch taken
With her ears ringing out in nonsense
Tears fall like rivers or a stream
Sweat gathering upon her palms
As she releases the secrets of the dark

The ache

Aching hearts
Tempered like
Fragile glass
And coiled like
Old rusty nails
Hearts of stone
Unpure – rotten
Sculptured
On show and
Insanely ugly – yet
Immensely void
In worlds apart
A poise and distressed
Raw – yet
Beaten half ruptured
A heart-filled hole
Of fragility

Lighting the way

In darkness we see
The light shining upon us
Now we see our path

In that, you preach

Empty spaces
In that, you preach
Places in-between
She sits
Ushered into silence
Afraid of her own voice
Of repercussions
Led by those who preach
Tomorrow is the day
The one where she's
Made to perform, like monkey's
For a cruel audience
In that, you preach
For her worth, yet not
Her own worthiness
Of the only way, your way
Her little life – ready
To be owned by you
Masks hiding
A multitude of sins
In a shameful existence
In that, you preach
For her worth, yet not
Her own worthiness

If only

If only you would stop
Before you started
Instead, you took from me
A power, unreturned
An innocence lost
In some place unvisited
You were not ill
Nor was you diseased
Yet you were to be looked up to
Like other's dads
Though you were different
If only you saw the error
Of your wayward ways
Admitting wrong doings
Or just didn't do it...full stop
I wrote many a letter – unposted
Yet burnt
I'd ask why? Why me?
You would beg for forgiveness
A sorry may have sufficed
Though
Moments passed
Years gone by
With only one thing left to say
I survived

Someone to fear

My voice echoed
Through the chaos
Of whom you are
My eyes distorted
By you, someone to fear
The terror you caused
You used me
You abused me
No care – I say no
But I wouldn't dare
Fear shown through
Stain glass windows
In crevices, blood
Inscribed a date
A time I was going to die
Locked away – left
A time to think
To fight
For the little
Life left inside of me
With minutes
No time
And left with one choice
To fight back
Until I could win back
My life
A freedom
Yet – I did

Find me in the gantry

Find me in the gantry
As I hide from humankind
Following inhumane
Acts of terror against me
Lips sewn shut
Follow my trail
Bleeding from
Unearthed wounds
Unseen through naked eyes
A poorly beating heart
Just, won't you hurry
Find me in the gantry

The playground

The playground
A home where bullies roam
And teachers turn blind eyes
To children's single cries
And kids panic-run
The playground
Where swings were dominated
By the ringleader
And his sidekicks
Who takes control
You see as bullies roam
Looking deeply
The playground
Full of kids who cry out
For the adults
To show them the way
And how to behave
Little by little
The playground
A place where bullies once roamed
The children's cries are joyful
And the swings
For all to play
The playground
A home to where kids are kids
And a generation
Becomes one

Dismissed

You
Lied to
All who would
Listen, while culled
Kicked to the kerb, you
All tried to destroy me
A question of why? I asked
Again, dismissed, and unanswered
Torture remaining and residing
In a place not to deploy or evermore
She remains willing to tell her story
No lies be told, nor to be believed
Bruises and physical scars heal
Yet she hides what is believed
To hide her ghastly, once
Removed and she gains
Strength and power
Stolen like
Her soul
Freed

I have a hunger

I have a hunger
For the way you
Glance at me
With perplexion in your eyes
A perception being ebbed
Safe in you – she smiles
I have a hunger
For survival
Of unseen trauma
And mysteries unsolved
Faltering senselessly
A hunger, yet not for food
But a life, a life without sadness
Or hatred, a hunger – she sighs
I have a hunger
For a world filled with peace
A place a heart desired
Somewhere to unite
To call home
I have a hunger
For the way I survived
And told the truth
Enough to tell my story
I have a hunger
A hunger for
Life

Five bridges crumble – Journey to home

Crumbling life
Begging, she starves
Of her own future
Breathing in silenced
Heartbeats – she pauses
Five bridges
She wanders
In aimless wonder
A world hers
While fear hurts
Emotionless
Possibilities gone
As days go into weeks
Weeks into months
And…
Months into years
Searching, she moves
House to house
To cities and her
Five bridges crumble
Her journey to home
She finds her own peace
Her sanctuary
And no longer in solitude

These words

I paint my life as perfect
As I hide my flaws
A blame I hold close to me
While I cry behind closed doors

A secret taken to his grave
The day it got revealed
A truth I told, a lie he beholds
No longer can it stay concealed

Yet, through the decades of my life
I live in utter shame
Those cutting words in my ear
You're the only one to blame

Now I need to take control
And live my life again
You tried and failed one last time
As you caused me so much pain

Now I'm seeking all the help
To put right all your wrongs
I need to put some ghosts to rest
And make life a beautiful song

I will leave you with these words
As you rot beneath the earth
I'm living a life you almost took
And yes, now I know my worth

The things they said

They said I couldn't
But damn right I did
They said I should be dead
Look at me – I'm alive
They broke me down
While I built myself up
I AM ME
Doing all
I CAN and WILL
To survive
On my own
I did all they said I couldn't
I survived when science and adversity
Meant that I should have died
At the hands of YOU

Was it worth it?

Was it worth it?
When you thrust her
Trampling on her soul
Until only a fragment
Of a life existed

You escaped justice
Allowing for her
To own a blame
And shame
Put on her by you

She must now fix her soul
Shattered by your control
And your thuggish ways
She begged for life
Now, trying to find her own way

Was it worth it?

Hope

Mystical mountains magically
Appear as a steeple of hope
And courage
She fiercely climbs
Conquering, calmly and curiously
In her wonder
As she unearths
Deep darkness within
Pulling at her soul
Capturing real beauty
In search of peace
…Breath…
Illuminating skies – inspiring
A world
Filled and fuelled with fortune
A world
Where love lives
…Hope…

Stepping out

Stepping out
In comfortless
Echoes whispering
In sheer satin glows
Heart beating
Rapidly as
The chest allows
Forbidden stance
With memories
Reborn into truths
Unhidden
As tears refuse to flow
Why won't she allow
Her vulnerability to show?
Hear echoes
Whispering, it's ok

Trapped

Running through debris-strewn sewers
Chains dragging her soulless body down
With blood sweeping through her veins
And sweat accumulating throughout her body
She hears of whispers calling her name
And feelings of shivers, felt
Haunted by a voice, heard once before
Her world filling with fear and brutality
As her breathing becomes laboured
Suddenly filled with adrenaline
As she reaches out to her inner child's voice for answers
Hearing her say…almost there, keep looking ahead
But do not quit, one said
Slowly picking up pace and strength
The chains begin to fall
Breathing now pure calmness
Ahead, something else
A light, open spaces, and life
The end of a nightmare – near
She is a survivor, nonetheless

Pandora's box

She dares to hope
To believe in good
Brave hearts
Yet to open
Pandora's box
With fear strewn
Across her face
Like opening a can of worms
Her truth
All the scars exposed
Telling of secrets
And untold truths
Her life once destroyed
Yet her courage
Helps place the lid
Back onto pandora's box

Unwritten rules

Unwritten rules
Of a child abused
It may be in the past
But it happened to me
I can't just get over it
This is me and who I am
I ask for no pity
But understanding
These are the
Unwritten rules
Of a child abused

They call me

They call me
By a different
Name each day
Unpleasantry's
Making me less
Of me, I say
As I sink
Into darkness
Into self-belief
That these names
Are true of me

They call me
Not one but many
A name for fun
My head bowed
In shame with no name
When I just want to run
And hide, and stay away
Hidden in plain sight
To rid myself of pain
Inflicted within my mind
It's time to re-own my name

Grounded

A symbol
Of life and death
Roots fragile
Like her heart
Laid bare a soul
Resting within
An emblem of hope
Proof, she fought
She survived
With broken off roots
Ready for new growth
Here right now
A symbol of beauty
Of life lived
And then death

Spoken

Smothering of words
Spoken with sweetness dripping
From her lips, she speaks

My tranquillity

Seeing my reflection
In the eyes of inception
Fixated upon the realities
Of change and colour
A path of direction
Of pain endured
Regaining a conscious mind
A glare as permanent
As inception
In the reflection I'm seeing
Moving from a beginning
To end with tranquillity

The serpent in you

I aspire yet
Not for your beauty
It does not exist
Though a touch
Behind a mirrored reflection
Aspirations failed me
For your serpent tendencies
To suck the life from my soul
I aspire yet
But the opposite of you
To be me and more
Without the bits of me
You unkindly destroyed
I'm not a mirrored image
Of what stands in front of me
You aspire to be a wrongun
While I aspire to be me

Silver linings

Silver linings
Lay beautifully
In the stillness
Of moving clouds
Floating above
Perfection
Of pure joy
In its wondrous
Beauty

Leather belts

As she pulls back the curtains
To the beatings and betrayals
Leather belts or clenched fists
Appear, while collapsed on the floor
Bruised, she sits paralysed by fear
Voices and laughter
In the next room
While her screams dismissed
Rejected by a life removed
Her courage misplaced – non-existent
She bled through whispers
Of words unspoken and
Truths forbiddingly told

A cup half full

Her cup
Half full
Yet, emptying, unsatisfied, frozen by fear
Attempting to make peace with her mind
Taking time
To breath
And regulate

Child's play

As she lay
Curled up
Like a baby
In the womb
Of her mother
Staring into a void
Fear pinning her down
Not feeling
Though –
Consciously awake
She freezes
Seeing herself
A child
Sweet little girl
With the world
On her tiny shoulders
At six maybe seven
An innocence
Taken to the games
Adults play, too adult
For her tiny body
An hour passes
Her aching heart
Tears locked away
As she carries on
With her darkest day

The things I didn't say

You don't belong here
In my room, you live
Between the walls
Inside my mind
Where fear cannot survive
Though, it's a place that I hide
I wish I had said
There's no place here
For the terror you caused
For the monster you became
And for the shadows you created
I feared the creature before me
Today I am fear
Tomorrow I steer clear
Of the moments in me of
The things I didn't say

Oh, honey

Close your eyes
And feel
Time no longer
Standing still
Oh, honey
Don't worry
You are safe now
It's your turn

Turn around
And see and feel
Your beauty
Scars on show
Oh, honey
Smile now
Hearts mending
Soul surrendering

Take a chance
And feel
Look around
Wind in your hair
Oh, honey
Life was so unfair
But look at you now
Just look at you now

Oh, honey you survived
The cruelty in your path
You took a chance
You look and see and feel
Hearing your own voice
Cheering and chanting
Keep moving forward
Remember the warrior in you

Love me not

To love me or not
I loved you
But you loved me not
I loved in ways
That wasn't right
According to most
Here I stand
Waiting and wishing
Hoping and praying
That one day
You may love me
But still, you loved me not
I showed you how
In the most unloving of ways
I needed what wasn't mine
Though, you didn't waiver
Telling me that
You will always
Love me not

Holding space

Holding space
For you
In enveloped arms of tight holds
I'm hearing you and seeing you
Your pain
Of brokenness
Will repair

Don't ask her why

Souls – empty
Destroyed with
Words and actions
And your betrayal
Being – Invisible
You did this to her
Feeling unnoticed
Like disappearing, a desire to die
Hearts – a shattering
Like shards of glass
Unrepairable, gone, broken
Like the trust she had in you
Don't ask her why
Don't ask for a forgiving heart
Remember who broke it
Those words, those actions
A feeling of invisibility
You caused a feeling of brokenness
Left confused – lost
She will wander through life
Her whole being transparent
But
Don't ask her why

Through the looking glass

Through a crystal ball
She wishes for peace
For a freedom of speech
Yesterday's truth
Today's future
And the kindness
Held within your heart
To rid all hatred
Becoming happy

I see you

I see you through
Sun gazed eyes
Endearing and presuming
Of innocence through thee
I speak with a quiver
To behold you
Keeping you near
In the face of change
I see you
Yet, I can't hear

Love

Be hope
When hope is gone
Be strength
When weakness is felt
Be courage
When someone feels fear
Be the kindness
We all need

Becoming one

A weaving of souls
Entwined as one
Thus harbouring
Secrets of such beauty
Yet, in a quandary
She seeks to untwine
The weaving of souls
Becoming one

Badge of honour

Suffice to say
She won
Becoming a warrior
And her own saviour
She wears her scars
With pride, like
A badge of honour

Locked away

You locked her in a cupboard
When you knew all her fears
In the darkness and all alone
Her fears unfold within her soul
And her cries and screams ignored
So desperately wanting to be freed
Locked away and out of sight
The memory fades over time
Though, the fear still resides within

I love you

Take me or leave me
I'll leave it up to you
Just know that
When I say I love you
It comes from
The deepness of my soul
I leave myself open
In the hopes you will
Be careful not to
Trample on my heart
I expect little back
But the same love from
The deepness of your soul

Turning pages

Turning pages
Starting over
Chapter and verse, middle and end
Erasing bad apples, trauma to heal
Ground yourself
Eyes closed
And breath

The therapists room

Sitting hyper-vigilantly
Opposite you
Afraid to speak, to trust you
To realise a motive in you
And yet
My feelings
Were right

Now – Can you see?

You capture the beauty
In time trapped by the sun
You see shapes misunderstood
For dark silhouettes
You wander beyond the stars
Like an endless glimmer of hope
You can't teach dogs old tricks
When all you see is fear
Yesterday, today, and tomorrow
You will see beyond here
Misconceived as terror
You will be that endless glimmer of hope
When you look beyond those stars
You will capture the beauty
With or without time trapped by the sun
You will see shapes
Not misunderstood for dark silhouettes
You will see yourself
Taking steps to heal yourself of pain
Now – Can you see?

We as humans

From nothing to seeds
That flourish beauty
A repeating cycle in a lifetime
Of wonder and be-wilderness
Tears fall in all seasons
As the heart beats
Like thunder in the storms or
Gentle patting in the sunshine
We as humans
Appear from nothing
But a single seed
Wishing to be left to flourish
Into beauty and wonder
She stands alone, upright
Waiting for the colour to bleed
Ready to fall below heavens floors
All set to appear from nothing
But a single seed

Sweet goodbyes

Shallow whispering
Sweet goodbyes
As you stumble into the light
That shines to guide us inwards
Like blossoms
Capturing beauty
Creating energy

What did you think would happen?

Would I lay down and let myself die
Roll over and give in to each punch
No broken bones didn't mean I wasn't broken
If you stripped me bare, hair, skin and fibres
What would the world really see

Look closely

A shell or just a skeleton? No!
The world would see brokenness, bruised bones
A broken heart with a fist shaped indent
A head full of blows and pain
Look past the image and imagine

Close your eyes and feel

My pain, my problem so I'm told
The uterus scarred – should be sacred
My brain carrying guilt and shame
Keep looking for signs of strength
Please keep inspecting my rawness

But then…

I found strength to climb
I replaced each layer of my being
I did not let myself die
I gave up taking more pain

So – What did you think would happen?

Trigger

You held her down
Preventing her from breathing
At a cost, you feigned
The audacity of your actions

Pinned down
Her silent screams while
Pain thrust upon her
But nobody saves her

Scars, torture
And broken souls
No fast cars
But a death sentence

Dying inside
Her mind full
Words, actions
Roleplaying in her head

It won't be long
Time to give in
Give up and leave
This pain is too much

You took her soul
Everything in her, you took
The only thing left
Was her tiny shell

A smell forced into her lungs
The taste overwhelming – strong
Choking her all over again
Even when she said – NO

Please don't pull the damn trigger

You almost pulled the trigger
On a life you tried to end
Her life survived and
Her soul eventually came alive

I promise

Feeling temporary
Is temporary
I promise the darkness will disappear
Revealing sunshine and rainbows and beauty
Just remember
Feeling temporary
Is temporary

How it all started

Let me tell you how it all started – from the beginning
From being a very small child.

You see…
I trusted and gave my all
To those who should have given their all - but didn't

Instead…
Their all was the opposite of love
It was a power thing, a control thing - It was hate

Because of this…
I grew up emotionless and empty
And I soon lost myself - death was a better option

You see…
As I grew up, pained from the abuse
The beatings, but I still loved them - It's all I knew

All the while…
I begged, I said no more, and I tried to run
I wasn't a good child, that was their excuse - but I was good

All that I was…
I was a typical kid, getting into mischief and scrapes
Doing all the things I knew I shouldn't - but I didn't deserve
A beating

Now…
I struggle with trust and self confidence
I love the way that I do, because of my abuse - it's special
Still…
I'm alive because I'm stronger than I thought
I give my absolute all because I have known pain - I'm
Surviving

What makes me, me?...
I'm unique but fearful of so much
Abandonment and rejection - but all this make me, me

Finally...
I'm re-writing my life - in a book
Taking back control – I will continue to love the way I do

Here is how it all started

There is no place here

There is no place here
For the beatings that never end
For the abuse, it must stop
Just like that, in what felt a lifetime
Hell was in a way behind her
It was in her way

There is no place here
For the damage one may cause
For the silent cries within her soul
Those are the cries desperately
Trying to be heard, but are not
They are ignored

There is no place here
For the pain one may inflict upon another
For the harshest of words yelled
And the cowering in corners
In the darkest place
She should have called home

There is no place here
On this planet and in this world
On earth where pain should not exist
But pain does exist, along with hate
Don't tell her to leave
Or get out today, tonight or now
There is a place in heaven
For she was beaten to death
Raped and abused, then she died
How could she survive this strength
How could she fight back against you
Tell me how?

There is no place in heaven for you

For those who ignored her cries
Or for beating her black and blue
She cowered in darkness
Afraid to breath
So, she gave in to all her pain

There is no place here for you

I remember

I remember the beat of my heart
Beneath your heavy breathing
Cigarette smelling breath
Mixed with your aftershave
As though you'd showered in the stuff
As my chest rises but refuses to fall
The ticking of the clock and squeaking floor
Time is almost upon me as much as you will be

I remember how you made me feel
In those moments of fear and resistance
I did not say no, yet you took me anyway
You bought me and took what your greed allowed
You knew my pain but my pain turned you on
Turning up the heat, your urges became more
Why? I asked myself, was I to blame…
Tell me
No blame, no shame lies upon my heavy shoulders

I remember the ending, the day I became free
But, I'm not really free of the demons
You employ to keep me stuck in a life you created
I look at this screen, at the words that I bleed like tears
Did this happen to me or someone else, someone stronger
You did this, you made me doubt everything…YOU
The pain I felt and the way my body reacted
I just don't understand what really happened

I don't remember you asking my permission
Nor do I remember you saying sorry
You did not admit that you were wrong
Yet, you acted accordingly –
Innocently
I remember times
I remember each moment
The moments that aren't blocked from my mind
Today, I remember that I'm innocent

Believe

If only
You knew
And understood how strong you are
You are stronger than you think
If only
You'd believe

It's time to Flourish

Don't be so sad
You have a strength, though hidden
Use that as your guide

Guide and glide your way
Through life with a gleeful smile
Your owning your life

Own your life and smile
In charge of your destiny
Carrying your own

Carrying your own
Standing up for what matters
Means your surviving

Navigating a life that's new

Don't think of my trauma with sadness
Or set some guilt and shame at my door
I don't take kindly to judgemental hearts
Think of me with fondness and so much more

Treat me with nothing short of kindness
As I navigate a life that's new
Don't tiptoe around my past
I'm still the same me, you always knew

I'll dance in the rain or snow if you like
Singing or swing and being free
As long as you treat me as well as I treat you
Only when you watch and all you see is me

Don't look at me with pity in the eyes
Count each blessing you have
No crying at the story I'm telling you
I'm here with you, lets sit here and laugh

Hold my hand as we journey together
I will gift to you in return what you gift me
Don't think of my trauma with sadness
I got this, we've got this – you'll see

Trust in me

To trust
In me
Takes a huge amount of strength
Listen to what your heart says
Let go
Of fear
And relax

Moments

In peacefulness
A sanctuary
Lies presence and hope and strength
Keep moving forward reaching your destination
Gaining power
Once removed
Taking control

Eternity

One kind
Of love
Between two souls intertwined as one
A love as safe as houses
Beating hearts
Treasured forever
Into eternity

Little girl

Little girl
Inner child
Meeting with voices in her mind
Dreaming as she visits this place
Don't hide
Little girl
Show yourself

Believe

I believe
In words
Bleeding onto paper like leaking pens
Creating chaotic beauty within the power
Of meaning
Feeling, seeing
Meaningful words

Remind me

Remind me
See me
Take me by the hand please
Guide me into a peaceful place
Without dread
Without pain
Just tranquillity

An opportunity

I saw
An opportunity
Leading me into my own survival
Holding my own, in scary worlds
I stood
And stared
I'm here

With love

Inspire with love
Words inscribed
In every hall
Every corridor
On every wall

We find peace
In the quiet
In the sleek
Lavish life created
No longer silenced

Loved moments
Freedom born
Into tranquillity
A place to call home
Showing kindness more

Inspire with love
These words inscribed
In each empty space
Showing up and
Saving moments sacrificed

This is love
This love
All that matters
All of the above

I swear

It's all over, my dear
Your safe, do you hear?
The days of fists flying
Of cursing your name
To those, it was just a game

Are you ready to smile?
Now my dear, it's your time
To find your hidden voice
I swear your safe once more
Taking the first steps, out the door

I promise it's all over now
Stand tall, head above the clouds
Get ready to repeat after me
I swear you are worthy
Damn right…I'm worthy

A story

There was a time of toughness
Moments living in despair
Tampering with a possibility
A freedom – A distant dream

There was a time of pain
Living with no gain
I was a child with no name
Trying to fix myself and repair

There is a day – Full of hope
A story behind my pain
Things were so insane
My death could not be in vain

Today's story is of my life
Not of my death
But of my survival
Of my beautiful life

Who knew

Who knew
When, how
Did you survive adversity, still smiling
Bringing new energy to another's soul
You made
History with
Your bravery

Perfect imperfections

Does perfect really exist
Amongst a world of critics
With judgement running
Through their veins
Like water
Each drip, a flaw
An unkind word
A perfected eye-roll
The daydreamer
Or the addicted and
The one who sees
Self-doubt, always
In a world of imperfections
Each flaw we see
Each flaw we feel
And each flaw we live
Are always, always
Perfect imperfections

This moment

Only once you'll stand
In the same spot
In this moment
You will not tread
This soil beneath
Your feet twice
Not only is this time
Treasured and measured
By each moment
Each movement
With each beating heart
This moment, always yours
Rekindle the love
Once standing afoot
Smiling right there
In this moment

Dear survivor/reader

*To those who may need to hear these words and to those
who think they may be alone!*

Alone is the last place you are, and the last place you'll
ever be. I say this with certainty because I was once you.
I was in the depths of despair, the grips of depression and
attempted to take my life but I'm here in a place of
recovery. I couldn't give up the opportunity to try this thing
called life! I'm winning, you can too!
There is hope of better and dreams that await you, you just
need to believe in you! Believe me when I tell you how
worthy you are, how worth loving you are and how strong
you are.
There is a big wide world out there, go and grab every
opportunity with both hands and live a wonderful life, you
deserve it.
Sending so much love to those who are finding this
struggle tough and lastly.
Be kind to yourself.
Be happy.
Remember you are never alone.

Debra X

Meet the author

Debra Reay is a survivor of childhood abuse; she is a first-time published author who has chosen to share her story through poetry.
Her goal is to reach out to and help other survivors of abuse, while helping them to realise their worth – In helping others, she can continue to heal from her own trauma.
Holding space for those who need it and being a voice for those who fear their own.
She will be a hand to hold and a light to guide you to where you need to be!

Close your eyes and take a deep breath – You've got this!

Printed in Great Britain
by Amazon